THE BURNOUT FACTOR ON LEADERSHIP

Managing Burnout in a Time of Unprecedented Change

April L. Ervin, MBA
Author

Enhanced DNA
DEVELOP. NURTURE. ACHIEVE.
Publishing Division

APRIL L. ERVIN, MBA

The Burnout Factor On Leadership
Managing Burnout in a Time of Unprecedented
Change

Library of Congress Number: 2020920391
ISBN-13: 978-1-7351349-4-9

DEDICATION

This book is dedicated to leaders around the world diligently working to sustain during these unprecedented times. Whether you are a CEO of a Fortune 500 company or charged with overseeing e-learning for your family, you are a leader in your own right. Each of you is navigating the delicate balance of maintaining all that is on your plate, during a time of extreme uncertainty. I feel your pain. I have been diligently working to do the same. These last several months have tested all I've learned and taught about sustaining our leadership and our lives. I have thankfully regained my peace through leveraging what some might consider unconventional leadership strategies. I offer this book as a resource to help you do the same. It is my hope that in reading, you too will be able to take back your peace. While we have been forever changed by 2020, I firmly believe we can still emerge with a sustained resilience and eliminate burnout once and for all.

ENDORSEMENT
By Dr. Simon T. Bailey
Breakthrough Strategist, Global Keynote Speaker,
Author of 10 bestselling books including:
"Shift Your Brilliance: Harness the Power of You, Inc."
www.simontbaileyinstitute.com/

Over the past two years, I have had the opportunity to support April as her mentor as she brought the vision for **The Burnout Factor™** to life. In our first engagement, I saw a *"spark"* and passion in April to use all she had experienced to have a transformative impact on the lives of others. Her commitment to transparently share her own journey of persevering through leadership and life challenges has powerfully impacted all in her sphere of influence.

When I first met April, she had just taken the courageous step to resign from her full-time position to pursue her life purpose. Having traveled that same path 20 years before, I intimately know the impact of boldly stepping out on faith to share your gifts and talents with the world. The result: innate brilliance is embraced, and lives are transformed.

The year 2020 has caused us all to face challenges and overcome hurdles never seen in our lifetimes. Through her second book: ***"The Burnout Factor On Leadership: Managing Burnout in a Time of Unprecedented Change",*** April offers keen insight on how we can sustain during these unprecedented times. April provides clear, practical guidance and daily strategies to enable the reader to persevere no matter how tumultuous life has become. Helping us see that we can emerge from 2020 with a new level of resilience. I celebrate April for all she is doing to help leaders eliminate burnout, decrease stress, and find greater peace now. I know leaders benefit greatly just by reading this important book, so very need at this pivotal time in our world.

TABLE OF CONTENTS

INTRODUCTION

To say that 2020 has been unprecedented would be an understatement. Over the past several months we have seen all we have known dramatically shift. Our lives, families, companies, organizations, country, and world have been forever changed. Our equilibrium has been imbalanced. All we considered "normal" is no more. We have been forced to not only think outside of the box, but to address extreme challenges when "the box" has been eliminated. There is no blueprint for this time in our lives. Professional and personal goals have been placed on the backburner, as we have worked to navigate an everchanging world. Many of us have been catapulted into roles we would have never imagined. Our former ways of working and living have undergone a sudden reconstruction. We are on a journey even the most creative mind could have never imagined. As we sit in makeshift offices in our homes, our definition of leadership and life have been forever changed.

Despite the hurdles, something within me still believed we could sustain during this difficult season. I know from personal experience that it is in times of extreme shifting that resilience emerges. Having been blessed to publish my first book: **The Burnout Factor™ On Education** in 2018, this year many shared: *"April we are experiencing burnout at a whole new level".* That consistent feedback was the impetus for this book. My goal is to help us know that no matter how difficult the path, we can and will make it through this time. I share my own knowledge and experience in the hope of preventing us from spiraling into a depth of burnout from which we would struggle to emerge.

As I began to write this version of **The Burnout Factor™**, the intersection of professional and personal became even more evident. Areas that have been considered personal issues to address, are now more prominent. With the exception of HR, these concerns are perceived to be dealt with outside of work. As we move through the most challenging period in modern history, I respectfully but adamantly disagree. I have always shared with my clients: *"what we do personally, we do professionally and what we do professionally, we do personally."* There is little separation. This is even more evident during this poignant time in history. Many leaders are now grappling with how to best support the mental and emotional health of their teams. The boundary lines of work and home have been severely blurred and for many are virtually nonexistent. Protective shields erected between the two have been dismantled. Laptops and computer screens are sitting on kitchen tables or in bedrooms. Multi-hour online meetings are now the norm. Attempts to shield parents and children in the background of Zoom calls have often been for not. The days of attempting to leave work at work are long gone. It is for this reason I believe many of us are experiencing a new level of burnout.

I've not been immune to these challenges. While I've spent the past several years teaching and supporting others to achieve greater peace, and *"eliminate burnout"*, I too have struggled. During a time of a global pandemic, physical quarantine, racial violence and injustice, political upheaval, and financial catastrophe – even my leadership coping skills have been pushed to the limits. Yes, the "Chief Peace Officer" has lost her peace on multiple occasions. But, I know **"we teach what we need to learn and learn what we need to teach"**. I have thankfully recalibrated and regained my peace.

By no means is all now perfect. But, as I have done in the past – I did my work. I was intentional in ensuring I did not allow stress, anxiety, and burnout to overwhelm my life (again). I went back to what worked. I pulled out the tools and practices crucial to sustaining me through previous times of challenge. Admittedly, my leadership muscles were put to the test. And just like our physical muscles, with diligence I became stronger each day.

As I regained my own equilibrium, I came to the realization that we are all experiencing a global reset. We have been forced to revisit all we've known and prepare for a future impossible to define. While unsettling, this time has been a blessing in disguise for many. We have been presented with an opportunity to revisit every aspect of our leadership and our lives. To *rest, reflect and reimagine*. To take advantage of extended rest, reflect on all we have experienced and reimagine our post-pandemic lives. While we may not be able to fully see the purpose in this time in our history, I firmly believe that new possibilities are emerging. Through my sharing, I am hopeful that you will began to embrace the same.

Sincerely,
April L. Ervin
Chief Peace Officer
Sustainable Leadership, LLC

CHAPTER 1: Managing Burnout In A Time Of Unprecedented Change

"Burnout is not about giving too much of yourself, it's about giving what you do not possess."

A 2018 Gallup study of nearly 7,500 full-time employees, found that 23% of employees reported feeling burned out at work *"very often"* or *"always"*. While an additional 44% reported feeling burned out *"sometimes"*. That means about two-thirds of full-time workers have experienced burnout on the job. *("Employee Burnout, Part 1: The 5 Main Causes", JULY 12, 2018)* . Just two years later, I can only imagine that percentage has dramatically increased. However, the type of burnout we are currently experiencing is reflective of a professional, cultural, and personal paradigm shift that has shaken our very foundations. I believe, if that study were conducted today, the burnout level would be closer to 80% - 90%. Many of us are experiencing a high level of burnout, stress, and anxiety as we work harder than ever in a time of extreme uncertainty.

This Gallup study further details that the core factors for burnout are: (1). Unfair treatment at work (2). Unmanageable workload (3). Lack of role clarity (4). Lack of communication and support from manager and (5). Unreasonable time pressure. Again, as we reflect on where we find ourselves in 2020 these factors have likely been greatly magnified.

The Effects of Employee Burnout

Employees who say they *"very often"* or *"always"* experience burnout at work are:

- 63% more likely to take a sick day.

- Half as likely to discuss how to approach performance goals with their manager.

- 23% more likely to visit the emergency room.

- 2.6 times as likely to leave their current employer.

- 13% less confident in their performance.

Source: Employee Burnout, Part 1: The 5 Main Causes, Gallup July 12, 2018

In 2019, I was blessed to speak to a group of leaders from a local chapter of the National Association of Female Executives (NAFE). During my talk, a man raised his hand with a question (I later learned he had attended the session to support his wife who was experiencing *"burnout"*, that's a good husband). As I engaged in questions, he asked: "Why doesn't the World Health Organization (WHO) know about your book?". I looked back at him a bit perplexed and curious. I responded "Well, I don't know, from your mouth to God's ears". He went on to tell me that over the summer the WHO (Yes, I'm aware some might consider them controversial right now) designated burnout a DISEASE. Let that settle in for a moment. *Burnout is a disease?!* According to the WHO, chronic stress and overworking were considered an "occupational phenomenon" resulting from chronic workplace stress that has not been successfully managed. Hearing that from that gentleman last spring, made me even more committed to my mission and purpose to help others eliminate burnout.

They further clarified that burnout was not considered a medical condition. I beg to differ, having experienced my own severe burnout in the early 2000's due to excessive overworking, exhaustion, stress and attempting to do it all. This had a significant impact on my health. During that season in my life, I exhibited many of the effects of burnout listed above. It was not until I had what I called my *"brick walk moment"* that all shifted. I hit a brick wall that forced me to change every aspect of my life. I received Divine intervention, as I struggled to change on my own. It was most certainly not an overnight transformation. My change was gradual, but ultimately lifesaving.

At a pivotal point in my own leadership career, I made the decision the cost of "moving up the career ladder" far outweighed the benefits. The sacrifices of working long hours, weekends, and extensive travel were just too much. Trying to be *"superwoman"* was just no longer worth it. My definition of success dramatically shifted. As I struggled with my health, going up the career ladder was just no longer my motivation. I was more motivated by trying to figure out how at the age of 35, I was 100 lbs. overweight and facing serious health issues. At a certain point, my doctor said these poignant words to me, ***"April, you have two choices: You can either find something else to do or manage significant issues for the rest of your life."*** My future and very life were at stake. Hearing those words, from my doctor, I immediately thought to myself, "What does she expect me to do?" I had worked hard to get to that point. And more importantly, I had a mortgage, student loans, and plenty of financial responsibilities.

With that top of mind, rather than heed her guidance I remained in that job for another two years. I rationalized that if I just hired more people I could better manage my health and work. As leaders, I am sure you can guess that was not the best solution. Despite my view of empowering others, hiring more people only brought more work and increased stress. Unfortunately, things did not get better but worsened. Two years later, I was eventually released from that position. Another Divine intervention. That transition opened the door to a complete professional and personal life transformation.

BEFORE AND AFTER: *BURNOUT*

Over a 7-year period, I thankfully regained my health and garnered a level of peace I had never experienced in my entire life. It is my own journey that strengthens my resolve to help others do the same. I openly offer my story as a cautionary tale hopeful that in doing so, I can help other leaders not travel down the path of extreme burnout. With all we are now experiencing, my passion for helping to end extreme burnout has only grown.

Many leaders I've been blessed to support face the same challenges I dealt with early in my career. Aggressively moving up the career ladder is expected. Working to the point of exhaustion is celebrated and worn like a badge of honor. But, at what cost? I firmly believe no level of promotion is worth our health. No amount of money, position or title can give us back lost time with those we love. With all that we have endured during this pandemic that reality is even more evident. Please don't get me wrong I celebrate achievement. I believe in success. However, we must achieve grounded in sustainability. To lead from a place of overflow rather than deprivation. So, just how do we manage burnout in a time of unprecedented change? Well, continue reading to learn just that.

Recommendation #1:
"It's Ok, Not to Be Ok"

During a recent team meeting, a colleague shared that she had heard someone say: **"It's Ok, not to be Ok"**. Those words stuck with me. Let's be honest, whether we lead a 5-person team or a global corporation nothing in our education or training prepared us for this moment in time. There is no blueprint to follow, no best practices to *"lean in"* on. No one before us has successfully led through a global pandemic, racial unrest, financial catastrophe, and political dissension that threatens to completely destroy the fabric of a nation (for those in the United States). There is no strategic plan to refer to. Our titles and status no longer matter when so many are battling a vicious virus that is prejudiced against no one. What we have been facing has touched every aspect of our lives, no matter our pedigree or degrees. 2020 has humbled many of us and tested all we have ever known. Our way of functioning, managing, leading, producing have been forever changed. Issues have been exposed and wounds thought to be long scabbed over are now openly bleeding.

As leaders, the logical route has been to immediately pivot and develop aggressive strategies to ensure we continued to move forward. While necessary, it has prompted some to act as if the pandemic were not occurring. There has been a fight to establish normalcy comparable to our former way of leading and living. While a necessary strategy, it has been challenging to do so without negating our current realities.

As we look into our computer screens, there are hidden pains that are not necessarily evident on the faces of those in our charge. While attempting to put on a professional face, many are continuing to wear masks not intended to protect from the coronavirus, but from current life pains. Some are silently mourning loved ones and friends whose lives have been suddenly lost due to this destructive disease. With social distancing, they have been unable to properly mourn. Our African American colleagues are emotionally drained by the continuous onslaught of videos of seeing one of their own brutally murdered with no legal repercussions. Other members of our teams are grappling with internal guilt for an inability to empathize or understand their pain. Many have been joining Zoom or Microsoft Teams calls having shed tears of anger, frustration, or anguish just moments before. Others in our charge are dealing with health issues unrelated but exacerbated by the pandemic. While others for the first time in their lives are dealing with severe anxiety and battles in their emotional and mental health.

As leaders we are certainly not immune to these issues. We ourselves are dealing with one or all of these crippling concerns. Doing so while attempting to ensure continued productivity, upholding, and uplifting the teams we lead. What we have been facing is challenging even for the most adept leader. This is why it is vitally important to ensure a focus on productivity, **does not** outweigh a keen focus on monitoring if those we lead are as "OK" as they can possibly be during this difficult time. If we are honest with ourselves, as leaders we are not OK. Let that settle in. We are not OK – and that is OK. I am here to give you permission to not be OK. This is hard. Leading during this time has tested us all. Acknowledging that, I want to also encourage you to believe we will persevere. However, to do so we must be willing to embrace what might be considered "nontraditional" leadership strategies. We did not learn these in college or business school. These were not the topics at most leadership conferences. In order to get to OK, we are going to have engage in some deep introspection and be willing to be vulnerable with those we lead.

The tagline of my business **Sustainable Leadership, LLC** is *"building leaders within"*. That is core to get closer to being OK. To persevere through this tumultuous time, we will have to build up our inner resolve for ourselves and those we lead. So, what does that look like? How do we build ourselves up from the inside out? We must focus on our own well-being, as well as, those we lead. We are going to have to move well beyond our leadership comfort zones. We're not just thinking outside of the box, we're creating a new box. I assure you that in doing so, we can and will move further down the pathway towards being OK.

Recommendation #2:
Take the Pressure Off

I am going to make a direct ask of you – **please take the pressure off yourself and those you lead**. We are navigating uncharted territory. Placing excessive pressure on ourselves and others, while untended can have a detrimental impact. None of us could have envisioned what we are currently experiencing. When we wrote our strategic goals for 2020, we could not have imagined trying to do so amid the unthinkable. Again, I empathize with you. As is my annual practice, at the end of 2019 I laid out specific goals for the coming year – professionally and personally.

As a visual learner, I placed my goals on chart paper and hung them on my bedroom wall as a constant reminder of what I was striving to achieve. Each goal had a specific timeline. However, as March 2020 emerged all of that goal setting went out the door. As I set an aggressive goal in 2019: *"To help 1 million people eliminate burnout by the end of 2025"*, every avenue to do so slowly disappeared. My in-person speaking engagements were postponed or canceled. The powerful leadership team retreats that had been so impactful in the past, were temporarily taken off the table. And on a personal level, my goal to get serious about a long-term, healthy relationship was brought to a halt. *(How in the world do you meet and date in the midst of a pandemic?)*. As I looked at my well-crafted chart paper, I felt as if the wind had been knocked out of me. 2019 had its own set of challenges, but I thankfully persevered. In doing so, many doors had begun to open in my work and life purpose. While this continued in the first two months of 2020, as the days progressed the closed doors increased.

Initially, I was determined to not let all I had planned go by the wayside. I kept pushing forward despite the obstacles put in my path. I soon had to face reality. I had no idea when those well detailed goals would be achieved. It was in that moment, that I decided to *take the pressure off.* I made the decision to rest in the current moment knowing that while my goals might not be achieved in 2020, eventually they would be. I just needed to shift and revise my timelines.

Admittedly, I mourned that reality a bit. My 2019 had a great deal of momentum that I fully expected to continue in 2020. After releasing the disappointment, I shifted my perspective and began thinking of ways I could modify my goals and still serve my purpose. Still hopeful for eventually hosting in-person speaking engagements again, some of my client agreements moved to 2021. Other goals were modified and could still move forward in 2020 (like writing this book). Client coaching meetings and retreats shifted from in-person engagements to virtual connections (thank God for Zoom – I think?).

While I eventually adapted, one important thing that I did was taking the time to acknowledge my disappointment. Doing so actually blessed me with a rejuvenated perspective. I better saw that even in the midst of what seemed to be unending chaos, I could still move forward with my passion and purpose. I would just need to do so in a much less stringent way. I had to re-envision my possibilities.

It often said that it is not the change that is difficult, it is the transition. When 2020 hit, like many of you I had to change – and quickly. However, as I'm sure I'm not alone that initial transition was a little shaky. Once I realized that placing unnecessary pressure on myself for goals just not feasible during this time, I felt a much greater peace. And, ultimately had the unexpected blessing of setting and achieving some new goals. I want to encourage you to do the same. I'm sure you are probably saying "Good for you April. But, that is easier said than done. We are pushing forward in our company, organization and home just to survive each day". Again, I completely empathize. In sharing this guidance, I want to help you understand that putting undo pressure on yourself and those you lead will only make things more challenging.

So, what are some practical ways to 'take the pressure off'? First, be realistic about what you and those you lead can accomplish in a single day. I always say that there are only 24 hours in a day, and we should be sleeping 8 of those hours (yes, 8!) and enjoying those we love another 8 hours. That leaves a targeted 8 hours to get your work done. I already know what your saying – 8 work hours?? Yes, it is possible to do so especially during this critical time. A tool I recently shared with a client team to make that a reality was "The Eisenhower Box". This was a simple tool President Eisenhower used to assess the urgency of what needed to be addressed on a daily basis. Now, if a former President can decipher between what is truly urgent and necessary, then we can do the same. In doing so, we are able to take some pressure off and give ourselves some time to "just breathe". I have my own paraphrase of President Eisenhower's quote below – ***"if everything is urgent, nothing is important".*** As leaders, many times we can elevate all to the level of urgency making it difficult to decipher the vital and necessary from the would like to have.

The Eisenhower Decision Matrix

"What is important is seldom urgent and what is urgent is seldom important"
— Dwight D. Eisenhower

As we continue to move through 2020, I encourage you to revisit your own professional and personal goals. I know it has been disappointing. However, in using this and other simple tools you can set some new goals and expectations for you and those you lead. In doing so, you will see there is still great possibility even in the midst of unprecedented change.

Recommendation #3:
Take a "Temperature Check"

I know this too is so not a very popular saying right now. However, this term predates 2020 and is something I've used for a number of years to assess how my teams were feeling and managing all on their plates. This is even more imperative now. We are all struggling and doing the best we can. This is a very delicate time in our work and personal lives. As leaders we must ensure we are actively and consistently checking the temperature of our teams. Yes, the irony of that statement is not lost on me. Prior to the pandemic, when I would sense concern or descension in my teams I would bring everyone together for a "temperature check". That was my way of keeping a constant gauge on their well-being. While some of those meetings were a resounding "all is well", other meetings provided me with critical insights I was unaware of. Despite living in the Midwest, my ideal temperature is *"82 and sunny"*. Some of those team meetings however were not 82 and sunny, but more like 120 and stormy. During these times, while taking temperatures might not be the best analogy, it is imperative that we are actively engaged in knowing where those we lead are on that spectrum daily. We must be actively invested in their wellness.

One way to do this is to hold space for your colleagues and team members through establishing a "Wellness or Self-Care Committee". This can be a cross-functional group within your organization solely focused on mental, emotional, and physical well-being. This group might consider holding monthly online "lunch and learns" inviting guest speakers to share on self-care, mental and physical health, or other topics relevant to your organization. The most important thing to do is ensure that those throughout your organizations and families for that matter know that you care and are intentional about ensuring their health, safety, and sanity during this difficult season.

In my first book I shared about the importance of taking a *"strategic pause"*. A time when we decide not to pursue any new initiatives and added work. I respectfully but adamantly share – **THIS IS THAT TIME**. At the time of my writing, we are in the eighth month of the pandemic. As we are an adaptable people, many companies, organizations, and communities have adjusted to our "next" normal. Our pivots, while initially disheveling, have been swift. When we were forced to leave our office environments we created workspaces in our homes. When we could no longer engage with in person meetings, we set up consistent calendars on Zoom and Microsoft Teams. Many leaders have settled in this place and created what is starting to feel like some level of normal. While the creativity and nimbleness has been impressive to see, there is a danger that we may not be fully acknowledging. If we continue to push those we lead to achieve productivity by any means necessary, there could be dire consequences that reverberate far beyond 2020. With all of these changes, it is even more important to focus on doing much less. New initiatives need to be tabled. We need a strategic pause. We must monitor the temperature of our teams on an ongoing basis during this time.

CHAPTER 2: You've Lost Your Leadership Rhythm, Now What?

*"If we get the right pace in our lives,
everything changes."*
– Pastor Michael Todd, Transformation Church

One thing most every leader can agree on – again whether you lead a global corporation or overseeing your daughter's kindergarten e-learning course – the pace of our lives has dramatically changed. Prior to the pandemic, most of us were accustomed to a daily pace of moving 1,000 miles an hour, often running on fumes. Despite the phenetic nature, we loved it. Getting up on Monday mornings to catch that early flight out became routine. Gliding through the TSA pre-check line as others stood in long security lines waiting to board planes. Grabbing the cup of coffee at the airport Starbucks and the barista knowing our order before we placed it. Being able to bypass other passengers and obtaining that revered seat with extra leg room. Or for other leaders, getting up and going to bed in the wee hours satisfied that our daily "to do" lists were completed. That has been our pace. That has been rhythm. That rapid pace was brought to an abrupt halt as the world shifted and our lives shut down.

We have been left trying to figure out how to live out this new pace. If we are honest, most days it feels disconcerting. This is foreign territory. As much as some might be grateful to no longer be catching that Monday morning flight, others are struggling with being homebound. The unfortunate reality is we don't know how long this shift will last. What we do know is that many of us have lost our leadership rhythm and are struggling to figure out our new pace.

Recommendation: #1
It's Time to Reset Your Leadership Pace

I respectively share with you, it's time to reset your leadership pace. Our former pace just was not healthy, nor sustainable. How do I know? Because that used to be me (and at times still is). I spent years running at 1,000 miles an hour on fumes. I learned the hard way that was no way to work or live. Recently, a client shared with me one of her team members said they were determined to find their new "forever pace". A pace for their work and life that could be sustained over the long run in the midst of all we are experiencing. This time of global shut down forced her to reflect on the fact that she needed to reset her leadership pace. That is my recommendation to you as well. This time in our lives, while difficult to endure has been a blessing in disguise. We've had an unexpected opportunity to rethink every aspect of our work and lives. Prior to this time, we each had a beat by which we worked and lived. I am with you on this journey. As my equilibrium has shifted, I too have struggled with resetting my own leadership pace. These months have deeply tested me as well. Know we are in this together. Despite the difficulty, I still believe a gift of this time is finding our "forever pace". However, we have to be very careful that we do not allow the pandemic to shift us in the very opposite direction.

A Case Study of an
Unsustainable Leadership Pace

How familiar does this sound? You are running on all cylinders. You have a 9 a.m. daily Zoom check-in with your team, your next call is at 10 a.m. but your team check-in runs over so you are late for the next call. You have 3 projects that need to be completed by the end of the day. You next call is not until 11:30 a.m. but a small fire comes up so the gap you had to begin working on your projects is gone. You look at your calendar for the remainder of the day and realize you have back-to-back Zoom/Teams meetings until 6 p.m. Guess those projects will have to wait until then. You also remember that your son has a soccer game at 6:30 p.m. and you need to drop him off at practice.

Once you return from the soccer field you can finally began working on those projects. It's 8 p.m. You have not eaten with the exception of a few snacks and half a sandwich as you drove your son to soccer. Your family has not eaten dinner either. You think to yourself "they are on their own tonight". You settle into your makeshift office in your bedroom working until 2 a.m. Once finished, you lethargically move from your desk to your bed – totally exhausted.

In what seems like a matter of seconds not hours, the alarm on your phone goes off – it's 6 a.m. It's time to begin your day again. This day looks eerily similar to yesterday – dejavu. You go down to the kitchen to make your coffee before anyone else in the house is awake. As you drink your coffee, you think to yourself is this sustainable? Is this how I am supposed to be living my life? Is this living at all? As you pose those rhetorical questions, I supportively share with you that the answer to all three is: NO. No, this is not sustainable, no this is not how we (I include myself) are intended to live. This is not living at all.

However, during this challenging time this is what our daily lives look like. For many this schedule was in existence even prior to the pandemic. The greatest difference is the elevated mental, physical, and emotional toll all of the things outside of our control are having. We must intentionally set a new leadership pace.

So just how do we reset our leadership pace? The first thing I recommend is to reassess what's really important in your life. I challenge you to take some real time for introspection and write down what really matters to you right now. Is it working 12 and 14-hour days? If you honestly take the time to reflect back on where you've been, I can promise you that there will be aspects of your former way of leading and living you will want to release.

Earlier this year, I was blessed to participate in the online Global Leadership Summit. As in the past, it was amazingly powerful and inspiring. This year, Pastor Michael Todd who I refer to in the quote above, shared some poignant guidance: ***"If you want true prosperity in your business and in your life, you need peace. Success is not just where you end up, it is how you get there. That is the pace of grace".*** I absolutely loved that - the 'pace of grace'. That is my hope for you. That you too can find your new *'forever pace'* and step into the *'pace of grace'*. As a side, I highly recommend Pastor Todd's talk. He gives some powerful guidance on how to do just that.

Recommendation #2:
REST

As we deal with the continued impact of this complex and painful pandemic, the best thing we can do to reset our leadership pace is to REST. I know that sounds simple. But, that simple act can and will make a world of difference. In my first book I share about *"The Transformative Power of Doing Less"*. That guidance still applies. When we take the time for appropriate rest, we truly are more productive. In her 2017 book, <u>The Sleep Revolution: Transforming Your Life, One Night at a Time</u> Arianna Huffington shares the importance of this very simple strategy. She dismisses the concept that getting little sleep leads to greater productivity. Amazon founder Jeff Bezos affirms this as well. He shares that he functions best on an 8-hour solid sleep and that shortchanging sleep to gain productivity is an illusion. I think they might be on to something. What do think? Amazon is one of the most successful global conglomerates we've ever seen. I know, I click on amazon.com almost daily.

Recently as I was preparing for a client retreat, I was searching for material to share on rest and meditation. I was surprised when a video of Kobe Bryant appeared in my YouTube search (God rest his soul). He was being interviewed by Huffington on the power of meditation and rest. He shared that during his basketball career he realized that his game was off when he was not well rested. Some of this revelation came as a result of his time being coached by Phil Jackson who taught the team about mindfulness and meditation. It's a short but insightful video, check it out. <u>Kobe Bryant - The Power of Sleep & Meditation</u>. In it, Kobe recommends just getting an extra 30 minutes of sleep at night can make a world of difference.

Studies indicate that deep healing occurs as a result of getting at least 7 – 8 hours of sleep each night. Kobe shared that he used to sleep 4 – 5 hours a night (sound familiar?). He realized and I hope you do too, that is just not healthy nor sustainable. As I share in **Chapter 5: Mind Your Physical Health**, healthy sleep has a direct impact on your body. Sleep impacts every aspect of our lives. As we contend with a constant onslaught of the negative in our world, it is even more imperative that we REST MORE.

Arianna Huffington has most certainly become one of the most significant voices advocating for the power of rest. In her 2010 Ted Talk she shares her own personal journey of working to the place of exhaustion resulting in a dramatic shift in her professional and personal life. I've deemed myself the black Arianna Huffington (smile) – great minds think alike! So, my encouragement for you as you think about resetting your leadership rhythm is to REST. Ok, I'll get off my soapbox, I think you get the point. It is just so imperative now more than ever that we get good REST. This is key to helping us sustain during these challenging times.

Recommendation: #3
Take a Technology Break

As many of us are continuing to work remotely, the use of platforms like Zoom and Microsoft teams have quadrupled. As we "socially distance" the need for interaction and collaboration has not decreased. As a result, most leaders and organizations have sought ways to keep their teams connected. And, if we're honest to keep tabs. With a subconscious focus on trying to know whether our teams are really working – Zoom provides visual confirmation that a work is being accomplished. I respectively argue that is a façade. A perception of increased productivity through technology.

Leaders and those they lead are exhausted. The impact of continually sitting in front of a laptop or giant computer screen is having a toll on our mental, physical, and emotional health. At the beginning of the quarantine the ability to connect "in person" even if virtually was comforting. However, as many enter into now several months of this reality, what was comforting for some has turned into fatigue for others. Zoom fatigue is a real thing.

Recently, as I was planning a meeting with a colleague that very issue was raised. While prior meetings had been planned for a 3-hour timeframe, he recommended we shorten the meeting to address "Zoom fatigue". It is my hope that some years from now, this does not become an actual medical condition. If burnout can be considered a disease, I can only imagine that Zoom fatigue might receive the same designation. In a recent Harvard Business Review article entitled, "How to Combat Zoom Fatigue", April 28, 2020, the author provides some key ways to address this:

1. Avoid multitasking.
2. Build in breaks.
3. Reduce onscreen stimuli.
4. Make virtual social events opt-in.
5. Switch to phone calls or email.

The article shares that our brains actually cannot manage multiple things at once (surprised to hear that? I was). That switching between tasks actually lessens productivity by 40%. As much as many of us pride ourselves on doing multiple things at once, there really is no such thing. As I have often burned my food attempting to cook, eat and work on two different laptops at once, I learned the hard way to just focus on one thing at a time.

One other recommendation in the article is to close all other tabs, programs and put our phones away while on Zoom calls. It is imperative that we FOCUS. The author also guides that when on extended Zoom calls, we can take mini breaks from the video. I know personally, I have turned my camera off out of necessity. Strangely, we tend to spend more time gazing at our own face. What is that about? I know I've done that. Even our backgrounds can be a distraction and overstimulating for the brain. It is recommended that we use plain and peaceful backgrounds or only have video on for those who are speaking at the time. I am all for that.

Another recommendation is to shorten meetings to 25 or 50 minutes to allow some break time in between (instead of the standard half-hour and hour). I also HIHGLY recommend building in "bio" breaks. It's astonishing to see how a basic biological need has been forgotten as we've shifted into our new reality. As we have all grown weary of being socially distanced, the article also shares that forcing anyone to be overly social right now is just not a good idea. At the end of the day, most of us are exhausted. We can't force social interaction. Making this optional is an excellent idea. It also allows those we lead to have more of a desire to participate when not made to.

I smiled at the final recommendation. While not intentional we truly have lost the art of just a simple phone call or text. I recall texting with a girlfriend and sharing we should get on a Zoom call. She adamantly said "NO!". Her work forced her to be online for 6 – 8 hours a day. She said, "just call me". Hearing that made me laugh a bit. What happened to the old school ways of communicating? We can continue to use them. I would also add one recommendation to this list. I highly recommend designating a no Zoom/Teams meeting day. Pick one day a week when there are no video conferences. As already shared, looking at our computer and laptop screens for hours attempting to engage as if we are in person is just not healthy. I promise you work will still get done. Actually, I believe more will be accomplished. Given the impact constant video has on our neurological systems, as leaders we must take the lead on this and set the example. Turn the cameras off.

Recommendation #4:
Set Healthy Boundaries

A huge issue that contributes to burnout is the lack of clear **boundaries**. During our current crises, boundaries have become nebulous. The separation between work and home is no more. Many of us have transformed our bedrooms and kitchens into makeshift offices. Or some of us have taken over our spouse's office and two are now sharing what was meant for one. One of the biggest boundaries that has been crossed inadvertently is our "welcoming" our colleagues into our homes. As we sit on Zoom calls, we often see spouses and children walking in the background, pets appearing on screen or elderly parents who have no concept of Zoom unexpectedly walking up in the midst of an important meeting (yes, I've experienced them all). While not intentional, this crossing of boundaries is having a significant impact. With a shift in our leadership rhythm, having no separation between work and home is taking its toll. The merging of work and home has challenged many of us.

So, what do we do about this? My first suggestion is if you work remotely, I encourage you to set up a physical boundary in your home and invest in your home office. Make a minimal investment in your sanity by purchasing some new office furniture and placing in a designated place in your home. It does not have to be expensive. The intention of purchasing something new is to show that this space is definitively for your new "home office". The other boundary that we must set is TECHNOLOGY. We must set a boundary with our technology. During this time, it is so very easy just to keep working on our laptops and computers well into evening. I encourage you to set a time each day when you shut it all down. I also encourage you to turn off the email on your phones. Being constantly accessible and attached to technology is not healthy.

In a recent article, "Negative effects of technology: What to know", Medical News Today, February 20, 2020, guidance s provided about the negative impact on our physical, emotional, and yes on our sleep. Some years ago, I shared in my e-book **"7 Daily Practices for Greater Peace and Balance"** (go to www.aprilervin.com for a complimentary copy), the chart below to help us release technology and get more rest. Many years later, this guidance still applies. I share again as a resource to help you set those healthy boundaries with your technology. I strongly encourage you to set a technology boundary. I promise it will improve your productivity and help you maintain your sanity.

Remove **ALL** technology from your bedroom	On that note, I also recommend removing all phones, computers, iPads, iPods from your bedroom – anything that distracts you from resting. **Arianna Huffington, CEO of the Huffington Post shared in her book _"Thrive"_,** that at a certain time each night she shuts off and removes all technology from her bedroom. She set the expectation with her team that she was unavailable during this "sacred time". _She does not respond to emails, phone calls, etc._ When I heard this, I thought to myself, now if a CEO of a multi-million-dollar company can do this given all of the demands on her time – **surely, we can too!**
Do NOT watch the news before bed (read a book ☺)	**Watching the news is absolutely the last thing you want to do before you go to bed.** Given all of the violence, tragedy, and turmoil in our world – watching the news just raises our stress at a time when we are trying to calm our minds. _(I know, I did this too!)_

Recommendation #5:
Take a Leadership Sabbatical

My final recommendation might be a bit of a stretch right now. I know what you are thinking before you even say it. **_"How in the world can I take a sabbatical right now, with all we are dealing with?"_** Interestingly enough, my

Pastor posed that same question to me. Well, my response is that despite the tumultuous nature of this time, it is still possible to take a leadership sabbatical. That sabbatical might not be 6 months or a 1 year. I completely empathize that is just not possible at this time. However, I firmly believe even two weeks or one month is still possible. Pastor Todd shared he took a 6-week leadership sabbatical in the midst of an unbelievably busy time in his life and his church. He allowed his leadership team to step up and oversee all that needed to be addressed during that time. He transparently shared he knew it was time, he knew he had *hit burnout* when he was extremely short with those he loved – his wife and children. It was then he knew this was not an option, but a necessity. Pastor Todd shared his sabbatical allowed him to have an extended period of *rest, reflection, and rejuvenation*. It also allowed him to be present during an incredibly challenging time in his family. Because he took the time to step back and step away he was able to **be present**. Being present is an imperative now more than ever.

As I attempt to practice what I preach, I find myself in need of my own leadership sabbatical. For the duration of this pandemic, rather than less I've had much more placed on my plate. And, while most of it have been wonderful opportunities it's been a lot to manage. As a result, once I complete this book I'm taking my own leadership sabbatical. Just a month off to focus on myself and rest, reflect and rejuvenate. In all honesty, I've been tempted not to do this. The opportunities being presented as I bring this vision God has given me fully to light, have been a true blessing. However, I know from experience if I don't do this now, I won't be around to enjoy those blessings. I must commit to taking a break, focus on my own radical self-care so I can keep my new *"forever pace"*. So, the ball is now in your court. When are you going to step back and take some time for yourself? When is your leadership sabbatical? Again, it might not be feasible to take a six-month break right now. Try 2 weeks, 1 month. I promise you that taking some intentional time for self will have lasting dividends.

Chapter 2 Reflections:

Take some time to reflect on your leadership pace prior to the pandemic. How much time were you traveling? Was the airport your second home? How well were you sleeping or was sleep optional? How much pressure did you place on your teams to maintain that same pace? Now, I want you to give yourself permission to use this time to develop and embrace a new leadership rhythm and pace. Develop a plan for your new *"forever pace"*.

_____

_____

_____

_____

_____

_____

_____

_____

_____

_____

My Plan to Create a Sustainable Leadership Pace

1. What specific steps will you take to create your new leadership pace and eliminate the aggressive treadmill of chronic exhaustion?

_____

_____

_____

_____

_____

_____

2. How will you shift your daily routine to ensure you are able to get sufficient rest? Remember, a powerful but simple strategy is to SLEEP.

_____

_____

_____

_____

_____

_____

3. How will you lessen the use of technology for you and your team? How will you set healthier technology boundaries in your home?

_____

_____

_____

_____

_____

4. When will you take your leadership sabbatical? Again, it does not have to be 6 months or a year. Set some defined time to step away.

_____

_____

_____

_____

_____

_____

CHAPTER 3: Mind Your Mental Health

"Every day, stand guard at the door of your mind." – Jim Rohn

Now, I recognize this might be a delicate topic. As leaders, we are not necessarily accustomed to or comfortable with speaking about mental health. In the United States, there most certainly is a stigma on this topic and it is often considered taboo in business and work environments. Despite the hesitancy to address this issue, I argue it is vitally necessary during this time. We are all experiencing so much pressure right now. As has already been shared, we are in foreign territory. There is no blueprint for this time. This pressure is causing substantive mental, physical, and emotional challenges. The pressure to attempt to maintain our work and lives as before can feel unbearable. And while we may not be exhibiting this pressure on the outside, I know from experience we are on the inside.

In addition to the pressure to maintain our work, teams, lives, and homes we are dealing with an onslaught of attacks on our social lives and psyche. Prior this time, social media might have served as an outlet to engage in innocent voyeurism and catching up on our friends' lives. Now a single click on Facebook might reveal that a colleague recently lost her mother and is holding a virtual celebration of life. We see the increasing death toll of a devastating virus, explosive wildfires, hurricanes demolishing homes and protests and riots due to racial brutality. This is A LOT. The combination of all of this is having a devastating impact on our mental health. It is imperative that we establish practices to combat the daily assault of pain, anguish, fear, and negativity on our lives.

As the late Jim Rhon shares we must "*stand guard at the door of our minds*". For those that are men and woman of faith, the Bible reaffirms the importance of this recommendation in God's word: "*take captive every thought*" and "*be transformed by the renewing of your mind*". Guarding the influences of our minds is critical right now. As has been shared, there is an onslaught of the negative that is bombarding us daily. With that, we have to be very intentional in how much of this we allow in our minds and lives. We can only digest so much negativity in a single day without it having a dire impact. The more negativity, the greater the difficulty. The greater the good the better we can manage our mental health.

In no way am I suggesting we walk in oblivion about everything that is being experienced in our world. Well, I take that back. That is exactly what I'm recommending. To mind our mental health, we must that take breaks from consuming all that is occurring in the world. I highly recommend taking a social media fast, as well. Take several days a week when you do not access it all. It's very easy to get caught up in reviewing our timelines. I get it. I do the same thing. However, I began to realize just how unhealthy that was. Additionally, sitting on social media has often kept me from remaining focused on what I needed to achieve (like finishing this book!). So, please give Facebook, YouTube, and Instagram a break. Instead engage more in things that nourish the mind. Read or listen to an uplifting book. We are dealing with so much tragedy right now, we have to be intentional about filling our minds with positivity and uplift. I promise you your mind will be better for it.

Recommendation #1:
Mindfulness Is No Longer an Option,
It is a Necessity

For the past several weeks, I have been saying this over and over again. As we progress through this unprecedented time, it is critical that we intentionally embrace mindfulness. With so much coming at us, we must work diligently to stay in the present moment. That is truly what mindfulness is at its core. To stay in the present moment and focus our minds so that we do not become overwhelmed by all occurring around us. Core to that is developing an understanding of the conscious and the subconscious mind.

Last year, after being recommended to do so many times, I finally read the book: ***"The Power of Your Subconscious Mind" by Joseph Murray.*** This book was lifechanging. It truly helped me understand how much our lives are dictated by the thoughts in our subconscious. For those that are not familiar with the difference between the conscious and subconscious mind – global neuroscientist Dr. Caroline Leaf shares: the conscious mind consists of thoughts we are intentionally choosing to think. The conscious mind only contributes to 5% of our daily behaviors. Whereas, the subconscious mind controls how we perceive life, how we react to situations, what we think about ourselves, and what we can accomplish. The subconscious mind is running 95% of our thoughts and literally dictating every aspect of our lives.

I was astonished by that revelation. I learned the very hard way that my subconscious mind was dictating EVERY aspect of my own life, and not in a good way. The results of my subconscious were the direct opposite of what I desired. For many years, much of what I thought about was the difficult and challenging. My mind was bent towards worry and negative. In order to shift, I had to make great effort to reframe my subconscious. To begin to shift the unhealthy thoughts running on autopilot in my mind. I highly recommend you do the same. Take the time to develop a conscious understanding of what is really going on within your mind. When we are not intentional in our thinking – when our minds wander, when we react to situations without thinking, when we are driving and realize we have zoned out once we have arrived at our destination – that is our subconscious operating on autopilot.

Studies indicate that our subconscious mind processes 40 MILLION bits of data every second. It is 1 million times more powerful than our conscious minds. So, if we have intentionally filled our subconscious with what we desire, that is wonderful. However, as is often the case our subconscious minds are filled with the exact things we do NOT desire. I can speak so clearly about that because that was me. I realized that many of the cycles I had been through in my life were as a result of my thoughts. When it is said that *"thoughts become things"* – that is so very true.

During the past several months, this has been even more challenging. With all that has been bombarded on our minds about the pandemic, coronavirus, social unrest, financial and political challenges – all of this has been seeping deeply into our subconscious. We do not want that. So, it is even more critical to begin to shift our mindset NOW.

One simple, but powerful tool is a program from Dr. Leaf who I refer to above. She is a world-renowned neuroscientist who has studied the mind for more than 30 years. She has a number of amazing books about reframing the mind. She also has a great online program to help us get all of those toxic thoughts out of our minds and input what we desire in our conscious and subconscious. The 21-Day Brain Detox Program (https://21daybraindetox.com/) is a simple way to reframe and renew our minds. I've utilized this program a few times. In her instructions she says that through this program we can eliminate 17 toxic thoughts per year. Now, initially that may not seem like a lot. But, believe me being able to do so can transform your mind and your life. I encourage you to add this to your toolkit to mind your mental health and embrace mindfulness during this unprecedented time.

Recommendation #2:
Meditate, Meditate, Meditate

Connected to a focus on mindfulness is meditation. Meditation has been life altering for me. Despite its powerful benefits, for some strange reason as the pandemic began I stopped my daily mediation practice. Thankfully, I quickly got back on track helping me to move me back to a place of peace, balance, and calm. By no means am I an expert. However, I have been able to use this simple practice to sustain my own mental health.

It didn't start out that way. Many years ago, my therapist (yes I adamantly believe in therapy) shared that she meditated for 2 hours a day. I was astonished. 2 hours a day? I thought to myself. I can barely sit down and be still for 15 minutes! As she provided me guidance on the benefits of meditation she also gave me a book: *"A Beginners Guide to Meditation"*. That was more than 10 years ago. I can still see myself sitting on the floor in my condo in Chicago looking out the window trying to "make" my mind be quiet. It did not work. At least initially. I kept trying though. I soon realized why meditation is called a practice, because you have to keep practicing over and over again. Now more than 10 years later, I've strengthened my meditation practice and it has transformed my life.

Meditation is like a massage for the brain. Taking just a half an hour to calm all of the chaos going on in our minds can make a world of difference. When we meditate we calm our sympathetic nervous system and activate our parasympathetic nervous system. If you are unfamiliar (as I was): the sympathetic nervous system prepares the body for the *"fight, flight or freeze"* response during any potential danger. On the other hand, the parasympathetic nervous system inhibits the body from overworking and restores the body to calm and a composed state. Through meditation, we are able to calm our sympathetic system and activate the peace of the parasympathetic nervous system.

Meditation has allowed me to better manage the peaks and valleys of life, the difficulties, and challenges without being completely overwhelmed. I can always tell when I have shifted away from my practice. My ability to cope, to respond with empathy rather than frustration is always evident. It is for that reason, that I HIGHLY recommend that if you don't' already do so, take up the practice of daily meditation. As I shared earlier with all that we are currently experiencing – *mindfulness is no longer an option, but a necessity.*

See the following simple meditation practice I use on a daily basis. In the guidance, I share how important it is to find a quiet space for meditation. That caused me to reflect on a time when my life dramatically shifted, and I moved back home with my parents at the age of 42 (that is a story for the next book). I was just getting into my meditation practice. Because I had little privacy, I printed and laminated a sign to place on my bedroom door to have some quiet privacy. It said: "Meditating Please Do Not Disturb". Without fail in about 15 minutes my loving mother would bang on the door and yell "Are you done meditating yet?!" There went my peaceful sanctuary. Nevertheless, I kept going with my meditation practice and even achieved that 2 hours a day my therapist shared some years before. Now that clearly is not feasible everyday but even twenty-minute *"peace breaks"* make a world of difference to calm my mind and, maintain my sanity and heal my body.

Simple Daily Meditation Practice

1. Find a quiet space for your meditation time.
2. Place a watch or clock next to you (I don't recommend your phone as it can be a distraction).
3. Choose a word that calms you. I often use "Peace" (no surprise Chief Peace Officer) or Jesus, Love, Health Abundance - whatever calms and lifts the spirit.
4. Sit and be still - as soon as you do your mind will begin to race. Let the thoughts come. As they do, think your calming word. You do this over and over again until the racing thoughts lessen.
5. Repeat this process three times a day for 20 minutes. That is only one hour out of 24 hours. You deserve that at a minimum!

Many CEOs and executives take their own version of "peace breaks" daily. The late Steve Jobs, an early adaptor of meditation described his experience like this: "*You start to see things more clearly and be in the present more. Your mind just slows down, and you see a tremendous expanse in the moment. You see so much more than you could see before.*" In the article "Why Leaders Need Meditation Now More Than Ever", Harvard Business Review, March 22, 2020, the impact of meditation is further evidenced in helping us deal with stress. Through meditation, we are able to calm our "amygdala", or emotional brain that manages the "fight, flight or freeze" aspect of our nervous systems. As we deal with increased uncertainty and pummeled with daily negatively across the airwaves, a meditation practice is vital for survival. As leaders focus on this practice, we can also have a definitive impact on our teams. If we exhibit a level of calm in the midst of chaos our ability to manage all going on within can actually shift the culture of our organizations. I firmly believe embracing this practice is core to being a strong leader. The ability to acknowledge that we too are just human and need techniques to calm our stress, will help our teams understand how vital it is for them to do the same.

Recommendation #3:
Seek Counsel from a
Qualified Mental Health Therapists

As the pandemic began, I was blessed with an unexpected opportunity to further my ministry. In addition to my business, I accepted a full-time position. (Thus, the reason why I am always focused on burnout). When initially guided to this opportunity, I questioned it. I now know exactly why I am in this role and the timing was just perfect.

Ironically, my first day in the office was my last day. I joined the team at the Christian Theological Seminary (CTS) on March 16th and we went remote on March 17th. I was in the office for one day! To say this was a unique way to start a new role is understatement. Thankfully, I was more than accustomed to working remotely. In all honesty though the longevity has even tested my limits. So, I empathize with each of you who are battling remote home office fatigue.

What I'm most grateful for in this new role is CTS' intersection of faith and mental health counseling. The seminary trains mental health therapists grounded in faith. Being a part of this organization strengthens my resolve for this next recommendation. We must seek the support of qualified mental health therapists to help us during this time.

Let me be explicitly clear in this recommendation. We do not have to be experiencing severe mental health issues to seek therapy. I am a huge advocate of therapy. Over my lifetime I've spent more than 15 years receiving support and am in therapy today. Is something dramatically "wrong" with me? No. However, what I do know is life can challenge even the most evolved person. As I shared earlier the "Chief Peace Officer" lost her peace multiple times during this pandemic. In addition to a new full-time role, I am an entrepreneur, author, speaker, minster, and caregiver. My plate is VERY full. Compounded with that is my mother's battle with Alzheimer's. All of this has taken a toll on my own emotional and mental health.

Despite all of that, my perspective on life has remained pretty positive. Some days I truly want to pinch myself for the joy and happiness I experience (that has not always been the case). How did I come to this place? I committed to my own healing. I took steps to ensure I could maintain this renewed joy and peace in my life, doing so through leveraging the gifting of those who have been trained to help others through life's pain and promises.

I encourage you to let go of any stigmas you have about mental health therapy. Seeking therapy does not make you weak or unable to manage your life. It's actually the direct opposite. Having the courage to admit that you need help actually shows just how strong you are. To realize we are not superhuman and we cannot do this on our own. In his article, My Four Habits for Maintaining Mental Health as a Leader, October 8, 2019, extraordinary leadership expert John Maxwell affirms that seeking the help of a qualified professional counselor or doctor is healthy. Yes, I agree it is extremely healthy.

During this time in our lives and history, it is imperative that we let go of any perceived stigmas of mental health therapy. I personally have three therapists that are helping me with very different aspects of my life. Again, by no means does that mean that I am dealing with serious mental health issues. I sustain my therapeutic relationships to ensure that I can continue to thrive in my life, no matter what challenges come my way. And, yes this pandemic has pushed that need more than ever before.

Embracing mental health therapy has enabled me to still have joy in my heart despite the challenges of 2020. Personally, I have experienced the pains of the pandemic, resurgence of trauma due to social injustice, shifting in my business and both of my parent's physical health worsening. And in the midst of all of this, most mornings I still enjoy my morning walk, enjoying the beauty around me, singing (singing is my therapy too) from a place of gratitude. That is the sustaining power of mental health therapy. So again, let go of the misperceptions and stigmas. Seek out a strong mental health therapist and counselor. You will be better for it.

Chapter 3 Reflections:

Reflect on how you have been dealing with your stress level during the pandemic. What impact has this pandemic and quarantining had on your mental focus and stability? How has this affected your work, life, and engagement with your family? Please know that no matter the difficulties, it is possible to renew your mind. Don't give up! Seek some help.

_____

_____

_____

_____

_____

_____

_____

_____

_____

_____

_____

My Plan to Mind My Mental Health

1. How will you leverage the power of mindfulness to ensure you can remain in the present moment?

   _____
   _____
   _____
   _____
   _____
   _____
   _____

2. What steps will you take to create a daily meditation practice? When and where will you take the time to calm your mind and refocus?

   _____
   _____
   _____
   _____
   _____
   _____

3. What steps will you take to find a qualified mental health therapist/counselor to help you sustain during this challenging time?

   _____
   _____
   _____
   _____
   _____

CHAPTER 4: Mind Your Emotional Health

"You never know how strong you are until being strong is the only choice you have." —*Bob Marley*

I'm not sure about you, but I can honestly share that my emotions have been all over the place the last few months. When the pandemic first began, of course there was great fear of the unknown. I recall being at my last in-person speaking engagement and hearing one of the participants on her cell phone. She had just spoken to her daughter who was at college and frantically asking her mother if she should drive home that evening. I had no idea what she was referring until I went online. That was March 6th.

In the next two weeks, like most in the United States my entire life dramatically changed. As shared earlier, I had great expectations for 2020. I set some aggressive goals which I firmly planned to achieve. Life had a different plan. As I grappled with all that was shifting, sadness and disappointment set in. And then, in full transparency some panic. I am a caregiver for my 75- and 73-year-old father and mother. We have thankfully had wonderful support from blessed paid caregivers helping me and my brother.

However, as life shut down all of that help quickly changed. The support and assistance I had for months was no more. I found myself full-time taking care of my parents fearing that they would be affected by this deadly disease. Exhaustion set in. Again, I'm sure I am not alone. Do you remember where you were when you first heard about the pandemic? Just like 9/11, I'm sure that day will be etched in our memories for decades to come.

What I know about minding our emotional health, is not doing so can and will have a detrimental impact on us. As we navigate a constantly changing world, it is imperative that we are strategic in taking the best care of our emotional health and to do the same for others. A recent WebMD article Stress Symptoms: Physical Effects on Stress on the Body (August 1, 2019), lists the core impact of stress on our emotional, physical and cognitive health. I share a few points of those points below. As you review these, I want you to honestly reflect on your own emotional health. This has been an unbelievably challenging time. We must be so very intentional about minding our emotional health as we move forward.

Emotional symptoms of stress include:
- Becoming easily agitated, frustrated, and moody.
- Feeling overwhelmed, like you are losing control or need to take control.
- Having difficulty relaxing and quieting your mind.
- Feeling bad about yourself (low self-esteem), lonely, worthless, and depressed.
- Avoiding others.

Recommendation #1:
Put Your Mask on First

I know, you do not need to say it. This recommendation too is a bit controversial right now (but clearly should not be). This is a recommendation I've used for myself and my clients for many years even prior to the pandemic. It has been stated on every flight we have ever taken. This guidance is even more important as we battle severe spikes in the coronavirus. It is imperative that we put our mask on first - literally and figuratively. We have to fill ourselves up first. We can't help anyone else from a place of depletion. *(Put On Your Own Mask First: The Safety of Self-Care, www.onbeing.com).* Again, this is not just important personally, it is fundamental for our organizations to embrace this mindset as well. As we traverse through this tumultuous time, please be sure that you put your mask on to protect and support your emotional health.

I'm sure you are asking, "April, how do we mind our emotional health when so much is happening in our world and lives?" Please know I am right with you. I've had to figure that out for myself. I had to determine what I needed to do on a daily basis to ensure a focus on what one of my colleagues calls **"radical self-care"**. So, I am sharing with you some things I do to put my mask on first:

1. Acknowledge that I am worthy of taking the best care of ME.
2. Be willing to put my needs before the needs of others.
3. Keep a daily gratitude list – reflecting on what I have to be grateful for in my journal each evening.
4. End my nights and begin my mornings from a place of peace – doing so by shutting out the noise of the world and spending quiet time intentionally focused on self-love and gratitude.
5. Doing what feeds my soul daily – walking outside, watching a movie, taking a hot bubble bath.

Those are just a few ideas to continue to manage your emotional health. I encourage you to develop your own list of what works best for you. If we continue to put our mask on first we can most certainly sustain during this unprecedented time.

Recommendation #2:
Just Breathe

My second recommendation in this area is to "just breathe". Breath is vital to our living. Without breath we cannot exist. However, many of us have been holding our breath for many years, especially over the past several months. Subconsciously holding our breath, hopeful this nightmare would end. Holding our breath as we try to navigate our new lives. That is the opposite of what we truly need at this time. When dealing with extreme stress oftentimes all we need to do is just breathe.

In 2019, a dear friend of mine wrote a book with that exact title "Just Breathe: Leading Myself One Breath at a Time" (Available on Amazon) which is included in the recommended resource list at the back of this book. She reminds us of the power of our breath. She shares that we should focus on a place of stillness, breathing in what we desire and breathing out what needs to be released.

This is a simple tool I have used in times of stress. During the pandemic, I've had to revisit this practice daily. To consciously focus on what I desired in my life, rather than what I did not want. I had to shift my mindset and intentionally catch my breath. Just this simple practice has gone a long way in helping me better mind my mental, emotional, and physical health.

A Simple Exercise to *"Just Breathe"*

Breathe in for 4 seconds/Breathe out for 8 seconds.
The breathing out is intentionally longer to fully release.

Breathe in joy for 4 seconds,
Breathe out anger for 8 seconds.
Breathe in peace. Breathe out anxiety.
Breathe in calm. Breathe out chaos.
Breathe in focus. Breathe out confusion.
Breathe in compassion and understanding.
Breathe out frustration and irritability.
Breathe in love. Breathe out hate.
Breathe in forgiveness. Breathe out unforgiveness.

The mind body connection is definitive. While traditional medicine has yet to fully embrace this, I am a testament to this fact. When are minds are in chaos, worry, confusion and stress our bodies suffer. One doctor recently shared that during this time the majority of his patients were coming in due to anxiety and stress. This was the case before the pandemic. Now it is greatly magnified. This is even more reason why we must focus on managing stress and just breathe.

Recommendation #3
Practice Active Forgiveness

As I have worked to mind my emotions over the last several months, I have thankfully been more successful than unsuccessful. However, I recently had a very emotionally charged situation. All my time of mindfulness, meditation and just breathing went out the door. Yes. The Chief Peace Officer lost her peace (again). Without going into too much detail the situation involved personal harm and while unintentional it was harmful, nonetheless.

I didn't handle it very well in the moment. Thankfully, I was able to take the time to release my anger, calm myself and take a long walk outside. Still at an emotionally high level, this situation affected my sleep and focus until the next day. Ironically, the very next morning I received an email in my inbox from Thrive Global on handling emotionally charged conversations. There are no coincidences in life. After reading this article and calming myself, I also realized that I needed to engage in a practice I had used for many years. I had to practice active forgiveness.

During a speaking engagement last year, I shared with the audience my daily practice of forgiveness. For some time on a daily basis I have said:

"I forgive anyone who has ever hurt me in any way, and I pray anyone I have hurt in any way can please forgive me."

Just making that statement, I would experience a physiological shift in my body. Further confirmation of the mind, body, emotion connection. I continued to speak forgiveness throughout the day which helped to lessen the stress and shift the situation. As I did so, I simultaneously received some other poignant guidance. Dr. Caroline Leaf shared how unforgiveness impacts the brain and can actually cause brain damage. Oh my God! That was the last thing I wanted to do. So, I took the time to rest my mind, continuing to speak forgiveness. Doing so allowed the stress to be fully released from my body and to get a good night's rest. As I believe it is never good to allow things to fester I addressed the issue with the person that next evening. While both offering and asking for forgiveness, I also reiterated that a boundary was crossed and in order to continue in the business relationship my boundaries and requests would have to be respected.

That was a tough couple of days because I took what occurred so personally. Doing so reminded me of another wonderful resource. Some years ago, I read the book <u>**"The Four Agreements" by Don Miguel Ruiz**</u>. After this situation, I reminded myself of the practical guidance in this amazing little book. The author shares that if we can adhere to these simple four life agreements we can achieve real personal freedom:

1. Do not make assumptions.
2. Do not take it personally.
3. Be impeccable with your word.
4. Always do your best.

In this specific situation I definitely violated #2. But again, thankfully, I quickly recalibrated rectifying the situation in a healthy way not causing further damage to my mind, body, and emotional wellbeing. Again, I know I'm not alone in this. In sure each of us have had some situations over the past several months that make us look like those cartoon characters with smoke coming out of the top of their heads and ears. The frustrations of trying to work, achieve, teach, learn, and just survive have caused volatility and strained relationships.

To help sustain during this time, I encourage you to follow my lead and embrace the practice of forgiveness. Release the anger and frustration just breathe and forgive. It will certainly have a positive effect. During these very stressful times, we must also address issues immediately to maintain our peace. Our sanity and health depend on it. Think about a volatile or challenging conversation you've recently had. How did you handle that situation? How do you wish you would have handled the situation? Who do you need to forgive? As you reflect I encourage expediency of forgiveness – your mind and body will thank you.

Chapter 4 Reflections

Take some time to reflect on your current emotional state. Think back about your life when the pandemic first began. Do you recall where you were? How did you hear about the coronavirus? How did you feel? How has the quarantine affected you? What in your life has been lost over these past few months? Give yourself permission to mourn and release what was. Then, begin to think about what is still possible.

_____

_____

_____

_____

_____

_____

_____

_____

_____

_____

_____

My Plan to Mind My Emotional Health

1. What specific steps will you take for the next several months to continually *"put your mask on first"*?

_____

_____

_____

_____

_____

_____

_____

2. How are you going to actively focus on *"just breathing"* to ensure you can sustain your peace?

_____

_____

_____

_____

_____

_____

3. Who do you need to forgive? Is there something you've been holding onto that you need to let go of?

_____

_____

_____

_____

_____

_____

CHAPTER 5: Mind Your Physical Health

"Take care of your body. It's the only place you have to live." —
Jim Rohn

For many of us, an unexpected challenge of the pandemic has been weight gain. I'm sure I'm not alone in this either. I call them "pandemic pounds". This is so not a term of endearment. Over the past several months, all of my healthy eating strategies were all but thrown out the door. Overall, I'm a very healthy eater. As shared in the first chapter, I am clearly a foodie and have used food in the past as a coping mechanism. Well, with the amount of extreme stress I've experienced over the past several months of 2020, I went right back to those old habits. The result: an extra 20 lbs. that I thought were gone forever! Grateful that it was not the 110 lbs., but disappointing, nevertheless.

In listening to a recent podcast, the facilitator shared that in times of extreme stress we all regress back to the coping mechanisms we used early in life. Well, mine came back with a vengeance. Thankfully, I have again re-calibrated (that is my favorite word) and gotten back on track with nourishing my body well. Thus, that is my first recommendation for you too.

Recommendation #1:
Nourish Your Body Well

During times of extreme stress, it is even more important that we mind what we are putting in our bodies. It is critical for us to nourish our bodies well to ensure we can sustain our leadership and our lives. What we put in our bodies has a direct impact on our thinking, clarity, and productivity. As I shared, I have put on some pandemic pounds which I am determined to get off. I will be blessed to turn 50 years old on December 15th of this tumultuous year. My goal: To be *"fit, fabulous and fifty"*. Beyond the additional weight gain, my commitment is to be as healthy as I can possibly be. But, first I must let go of those unhealthy habits. My vice: carbs. Well actually potatoes and French fries. During times of stress, I definitely overdo it on the carbs and engage in mindless eating. I soon came to realize there was a physiological reason for my craving. In eating carbs, we actually increase the level of serotonin – the "feel good neurotransmitter" in our brains and gut. This hormone actually helps us to feel calmer. So, that's the reason I feel so great after a plate of sweet potato fries?! While feeling good in the moment, staying in that place of craving is not very good.

Some years ago, a team I led wanted to provide me with a surprise thank you for conducting our off-site team retreat. We were in desperate need of respite and took the time to step away from the office and engage with each other. The day after the retreat, I came into my office and saw flowers and a gigantic basket of all my favorite treats (and some of theirs): 72% Ghirardelli dark chocolate squares, a giant tub of peanut butter filled pretzels, Goldfish and candy. While I truly appreciated my team's gratitude, I realized it probably would have been better to set those treats in the kitchen. I kept them in my office. Over the next few weeks, I enjoyed every morsel of those treats. I was in the midst of completing a multi-million-dollar grant proposal. As I wrote, I ate. While that formula might have worked for the project, as the organization was ultimately awarded more than $10 million in funding, it did not work so well for my waist and ability to fit into my clothes. Thankfully, as I have often done over my lifetime when it comes to food – I refocused. I got back on track with nourishing my body well and feeding my body both what it needed and wanted. I share that story because I know that in 2020, we are doing a lot of what I did a few years back. My encouragement is to help you too get back on track. Whether it is pandemic pounds or just needing to strengthen your physical health, this too must be a priority right now.

Through my journey of obtaining optimal health and losing more than 100 lbs., I've learned a great deal about what is best for my body. I've also learned a great deal of the power of proper nutrition and the futility of dieting. You name it, I've done it: vegetarian, vegan, raw, all meat, no meat, all carbs, no carbs, keto, keto green. I've done it all, and probably just in 2020 (LOL). However, as I settled back into my knowingness I was reminded of pivotal guidance I received some years ago: "all things in moderation".

A diet of extremes will only cause more problems in our physical health. A mindset of deprivation will only cause us to want what we can't have. EVERY TIME, I say I'm not going to have any more bread – I crave bread. So, instead of working in absolutes, I'm allowing myself to have bread in moderation. I'm also grounded in what I know works best for my body – healthy protein and vegetables – and a little bread and carbs. I also ensure I incorporate real, natural food in my diet. During this time, while easy to grab the next processed, bagged food in our cabinets, it is even more important to actually grab those veggies at the bottom of the fridge. For us to feel our best and sustain during times of extreme stress, it is imperative that our primary diet include **real food**. We must eat food that actually comes out of the ground rather than a can. This makes a dramatic difference in our ability to sustain during times of change and stress.

You see that I'm a bit passionate about nourishing the body. While it may not seem so, this too is a vital leadership strategy. As we focus on minding our physical health, what we put in our bodies can make a world of difference. Additionally, as we continue to battle the coronavirus it is our nutrition that is the game changer. The stronger we nourish our bodies, the stronger our immune systems. If God forbid, anyone we know and love is plagued with this virus, healthy nutrition is critical. Our immune system resides in our gastrointestinal system – in our gut. So, what we put in out gut matters. Another factor is ensuring we are getting the right number of vitamins in our nutrition. In many cases, we are able to do so from our food. However, when we cannot, I recommend taking good quality supplements.

Ok, that's a lot on nutrition. But, again it is vital and so very important during this time. In the chart below, I share some of my daily nutrition practices. Remember, our bodies speak to us. Our bodies tell us what it needs. This is what my bodies need. Think about that for yourself. Think about what works best for your body and commit to nourishing your body well each and every day.

My Daily Nourishment	
Healthy Probiotics	Kombucha, sauerkraut, kimchi
Nourishing Vegetables	Daily green drink, collard greens, organic spinach, butternut squash, cucumbers, green peas
Healthy Protein	Salmon, grass-fed beef, organic/cage-free eggs, grass-fed lamb
Healthy Sweets	72% dark chocolate, cacao, oat milk, flax milk
Healthy Supplements	Garden of Life vitamins, cod-liver oil, organic sea moss, liquid vitamin C

Recommendation #2:
Maintain a "Simple" Daily Exercise Routine

This recommendation is pretty straightforward and thus will be fairly short. I'm sure we all know the importance of exercise in "minding our physical health". However, the slight difference in my recommendation is my new favorite word "simple". During this time, I've focused on keeping ALL aspects of my life very simple, especially when it comes to my exercise routine. I keep saying *"simplicity for sanity sake"*.

So, that is my recommendation to you. Develop a simple exercise routine that can be achieved on a daily basis. During the time of the pandemic, core to my exercise routine has been my daily walk outside. As I shared, most mornings (when it is decently warm) I walk for 45 minutes to an hour before my daily team check-in meeting. During that walk, I added one other thing to my routine: singing. Now, I'm no songstress but singing out loud as I observe the beauty of the sun on my face and trees around me – feeds my soul. It is my form of daily therapy.

Admittedly, there have been many days I have gotten strange looks from those in my path. However, on the positive side I realized that my therapeutic singing was blessing others. One day, as I was walking down the street I noticed a woman walking her dog. I waved and said hello from an appropriately socially distanced place. As I continued to walk, I heard her speaking and took out one of my air pods. She said, "I hate it when I'm not on my porch and I miss you!" I thanked her and shared this was just part of my daily therapy. She went to say "Are you in a choir or are you singer? You have a beautiful voice." I thanked her and laughed a bit to myself. I can keep a tune, but that's about it. I also laughed to myself as I thought about my massage therapist asking me what I sang when I walked. I joked that I wasn't walking down the street singing my favorite rap song (at 49). Nothing wrong with that and no judgment, but as a woman of faith my song of choice is always gospel music. Many of these songs have kept me sane during this time of insanity.

Another day, during my walk a man across the street waved at me. Socially distanced, he pulled down his mask and said "You know I've been working on this house for weeks. I just have to share with you how I've enjoyed you. I heard you coming all the way down the street. Thank you". We never know how our willingness to take the best care of ourselves can benefit others. You never know who is watching. You never know who might be encouraged. In my sharing, I hope you too are encouraged to find your simple daily exercise routine.

This simple daily practice has truly helped me manage my stress level. I also learned there is actually a neurological benefit of this practice. In the article "The Health Benefits of Singing a Tune", Chicago Times, March 15, 2018, singing actually releases endorphin hormones which helps to calm the nervous system. Not that I needed further evidence to continue. It does reaffirm the importance of daily exercise in managing our stress and physical health. So, I will keep walking and singing – and purchase a nice warm jacket as the winter months approach in my part of the world.

Recommendation: #3
Ground Yourself

As many of us have spent days and months inside of our homes, the outside and our normal routines have fully dissipated. While not ideal, being in our homes actually presents a unique opportunity. As we sit at our makeshift desks staring out our colleagues and Zoom screens, we might wish for that long drive to work even in bumper to bumper traffic. Just, desiring to get outside. Well, I cannot say I've ever been a fan of rush hour traffic, but multiple weeks in my own home have even challenged me. My solution: grounding myself in nature. Get outside. For those who are blessed to have beautiful year-round weather, you have no excuse. For those of us who experience all four seasons and at times a heavy winter we have to maximize our warm months. During the pandemic that is exactly what I did.

My massage therapist (yes, I recommend this as well even with a mask and plastic gloves) shared with me this concept called "grounding" or "earthing". I wasn't familiar it. She shared that some years ago a former cable executive had developed a documentary of the health benefits of getting outside and grounding our feet in nature. He shares that we were never meant to wear rubber on our feet all the time. That placing our bare feet in the ground had healing benefits. I know crazy right? But crazy times, call for crazy measures.

Actually, as I was writing this book I went back to that practice. With my small foldout chair from Target, I found a quiet place covered by trees. I sat my chair down took my sandals off and placed my feet in the grass. I had not done so for days. I forgot how great it felt. Previously, I was a bit tired and lethargic. I now had a new level of energy and was able to finish this section of the book.

Don't take my word for it. I encourage you to watch the documentary: The Earthing Movie: The Remarkable Science of Grounding (available on YouTube). I just clicked on it myself to remind me of the power of this very simple healing tool. Having battled chronic health issues for many years, I am truly grateful for the natural ways to heal and restore our bodies. I also found out that there are grounding mats to keep under our desks and grounding pads to sleep on. I haven't purchased them yet, but they are on my list. Of course, like everything else you can find them on Amazon. (What is not on Amazon? My orders have definitely gone a bit overboard during the pandemic. But, these purchases are well worth it.)

Chapter 5 Reflections

Reflect on how you've been challenged in your physical health during the pandemic. Are you happy with where you are with your body and your health? Are you battling pandemic pounds? I know it's not easy. I encourage you to release the disappointment and frustration. Reflect on how you can make a change to better manage your physical health. Commit to doing better – you deserve it!

_____

_____

_____

_____

_____

_____

_____

_____

_____

_____

_____

My Plan to Mind My Physical Health

1. What changes are going to make in our diet to ensure that you *nourish your body well?*

_____

_____

_____

_____

_____

_____

_____

2. What is going to be your simple daily exercise routine to ensure you are getting your physical activity?

_____

_____

_____

_____

_____

_____

3. How do you plan to remain *"grounded"* to ensure that you are able to sustain your new foundation of physical health?

_____

_____

_____

_____

_____

_____

CHAPTER 6: Uprooting the Roots of Burnout

"We all have within us the ability to move from struggle to grace."
— *Arianna Huffington*

In this section, I want to get a bit more personal. In doing so, I am hopeful you can honestly reflect on your own struggles with burnout. The root of my own leadership burnout has always had to do with living up to the expectations of others and valuing myself based on what I did. I spent many years defined by my job, title, salary, material belongings, and perceived success. All doing so completely BURNED OUT.

Now that I've done my "inside out" work, I recognize this pattern is rooted in my childhood (isn't everything?). I grew up in a very volatile home (stay with me, I know this is personal). That volatility caused me to seek peace and pleasing others by any means necessary. I was able to do so through getting good grades, doing more, and being celebrated at school. When that happened home felt better. It felt calmer, more peaceful, and safe.

As I grew older, being celebrated for my financial achievements, possessions and perceived success brought a feeling of admiration. I felt better about who I was for what I did. This feeling and the *"disease to please"* impacted every aspect of my life, including my leadership. Constantly going above and beyond to ensure those under my tutelage were well taken care of, often taking my empathy to an unhealthy level. That inner desire to please others caused extreme exhaustion. My 8-year-old self subconsciously believing if she could just do better, things would be better, and the pain of the past would go way. Through my own journey of inner healing I learned that was not ever going to be the case. I could not work, earn, or achieve my pain away I had to heal my past. I had to *"face it in order to fix it"*. Thankfully, I have been able to do so. By no means am I perfect. Perfection is not the goal. My goal has and continues to be embracing my real, authentic best self. All of me.

I am so very thankful to understand the root of my burnout. It has taken work but, has been worth it. I respectfully ask, what is the root of your burnout? Take some real time to reflect. Your story might not be my story, but I promise you there is an underlying root. And with all that we are experiencing in 2020, these roots are coming up from the ground. This fact reinforces the importance of all that has been shared in the previous chapters. Whatever the root, I promise you it is possible to shift that reality and eliminate burnout once and for all.

Recommendation:
Take Something Off Your Plate

In addition to reflecting on our own journey of burnout, I offer one other recommendation. It is time to take something off of your plate. We all have a great deal on our plates – each and every day. This year has only expanded that. With already busy schedules, our attempts to continue to push forward during a pandemic has prompted us to put even more on our plates. As I have openly shared, I am in no way immune to this issue. As I attempted to meet my publisher's deadline, I realized I had way too much on my own plate (again). I am currently blessed with many opportunities. As shared, I currently work in seminary education, have a thriving consulting business, author, keynote speaker and caregiver for my elderly parents (just writing that made me a little tired – how about you?). You see again why I write about burnout. Again, **we teach what we need to learn and learn what we need to teach**. Back to the deadline.

As I diligently worked to complete this book, I also had a client retreat to plan and an upcoming speaking engagement within a 2-week period. It was too much. I had to take something off of my plate. Ironically, during the retreat, I facilitated a very simple exercise. We had two paper plates – one for professional and one for personal. I asked my clients to write down on each plate all of their current responsibilities. I did the exercise with them. As I shared my own plates – my professional plate was FULL. My personal plate, not so much. That gave me a revelation – I need to get a personal life! A bit out of balanced again.

During this time, I was regressing back into overdoing it and burnout. But, thankfully caught myself. My first signal is always how my body is feeling. My body is my feedback mechanism. Actually, it is for all of us. In the midst of my writing, I committed to myself to immediately begin practicing what I preached. Thankfully, I got a nudge from my wonderful publisher – a text message that read "I think we need to push your Book Launch back". Just getting that text, I could feel a physiological release in my body. She had given me permission to take something off my plate. I immediately felt better. She helped me take the pressure off knowing that the book would eventually be completed and shared with the world (as it has been). She also gave me a Divine reminder that I needed to do the same for myself. While I absolutely love all I am blessed to do, I must maintain my commitment to ensuring that I do not regress to the level of burnout that I experienced almost 15 years ago. Again, I encourage you to use my journey as a cautionary tale. During this time in our lives, we MUST take some things off of our already very full plates.

Chapter 6 Reflections

Reflect on your own life journey. How has burnout impacted your life? Do you see any patterns? What do you believe the root cause is? We are creatures of habit. It is in our intentional reflection that can begin the shift. Remember, we must face it, to fix it. Going within can and will shift our outside reality.

_____

_____

_____

_____

_____

_____

_____

_____

_____

_____

_____

_____

My Plan to Uproot the Roots of Burnout

1. What specific steps will you take to no longer allow burnout to affect your life?

_____

_____

_____

_____

_____

_____

_____

2. How will you ensure that you can sustain through the pandemic and beyond and not repeat the same patterns?

_____

_____

_____

_____

_____

_____

_____

3. What daily practices will you put in place to give yourself grace and take something off of your plate?

_____

_____

_____

_____

_____

_____

CHAPTER 7: Hitting the Reset Button, the Power of Resilience

"I can be changed by what happens to me. But I refuse to be reduced by it." — Maya Angelou

2020 has been a year of the ultimate reset. We've experienced dramatic shifts in our professional and personal lives. I firmly believe we must let go of any desire to "get back to normal". What was will never be again, at least not in the way we have formerly experienced. While difficult, challenging, and tumultuous, 2020 has blessed us with a hidden gift: The opportunity to *"hit the reset button"*. We have the opportunity to start over from a new, more strengthened place and state of mind. As leaders, many of us and those we lead are trying to figure out what our "next normal" looks like. If there is no going back, then where do we go from here. To answer that question, I again want to share a bit more about my own journey of resetting and gaining sustaining resilience.

I personally have had to hit the reset button multiple times over my life. As I shared, I started out very early in life focused on achievement. My parents deeply engrained in me the importance of getting a good education, doing well in school, obtaining a strong career that would enable me to earn a good income. Neither of my parents attended college, however they were adamant I would do so. I was blessed to attend Northwestern University for my undergraduate degree and an MBA from the University of Michigan. What was instilled in me from a very early age came to fruition. And then…..life happened. My pathway of success dramatically shifted resulting in multiple resets that ultimately emerged into a Divine life purpose.

Reset #1:
September 10, 2001

I'm sure you might recognize this date but might be thinking it's a typo. It is not. On September 10th, 2001, I flew from Chicago to New York for a one-day meeting with my former consulting firm. I clearly recall taking a small suitcase with just enough clothing for my meeting the next day. Like the rest of the world, the next morning I woke up to the unimaginable. I sat in my hotel room in midtown Manhattan trying to figure out what was going on and reach my family. I spent about a week on my girlfriend's sofa in Brooklyn in a place of stunned trauma. I was finally able to rent a car and drive from New York City back to Chicago. By God's grace – safe and healthy. This experience prompted the first shift and reset. My career transitioned from the for profit to nonprofit. With gratitude, something within was seeking greater meaning in my professional and personal life. RESET.

Reset #2:
August 2006

As I previously shared, I have been blessed to survive a pretty significant health journey. It was on this date, that my doctor said those poignant words that I needed to change my career or risk managing health issues for the rest of my life. Despite this clear guidance, it would take some time for me to act on her recommendation. As a result, on a daily basis my health and life deeply deteriorated. Despite this challenge, I pushed through and persevered attempting to maintain all that I had worked hard to achieve. My identity was wrapped up in my work. I subconsciously thought if I left my job I would lose who I was. RESET.

Reset #3:
August 2008

Fast forward two years later, and I experienced a shift that was life altering. One that felt horrendous when it occurred, but in retrospect was another Divine gift. It was this date in 2008 that I was fired from the position my doctor told me to leave just two years before. While startling, something within me knew it was coming. Just a few weeks before, I had taken a health sabbatical. I had spent the last week of that time with a dear friend at her condo in Atlanta. The night before my flight back to Chicago, she said to me "You don't want to go back, do you?" I looked at her with sadness in my heart and said "No". But, I still did not know what else I could do. Well God did. After being asked to fly to New York the next day (that in itself was a journey after 9/11), I walked into a conference room and was released from my job. I was devastated. As I walked down 5th avenue, tears flowed down my face. I was stunned. I was in that place for some time, and it would take several months for me to reemerge. Thankfully, stronger, and healthier. RESET

Reset #4:
November 2011

Fast forward three years later. I experienced another monumental reset that changed EVERYTHING. As I held tightly onto all that was, God was diligently working to remove it from my hands. In 2011, I went through what my Pastor calls *"A Divine Storm"*. In a matter of months, I lost everything I had built over 20 years. I lost my health, home, clothes, car, business, and finances. I went from "six figures to food stamps" and moved back home with my parents at the age of 42. Thankfully, I had somewhere to go. And, thankfully, that was only one part of my story. My entire life changed in a matter of months. So much so it made my head spin. In the midst of this monumental reset, I did not realize my life was being opened up to a 7-year journey that would transform my very being. RESET. (The full story of this reset is in my upcoming book: **"A Divine Storm: My Journey of Losing it All for the Restoration of My Soul"**). ULTIMATE RESET.

Reset #5:
May 2018

It was 7 years almost to the month of my first reset that opened the door to my fully emerging into my life purpose. At this time, I had the opportunity to work for a nonprofit organization that had a definitive impact on my life as a youth. While a tremendous blessing, something deep within me knew I was meant for more. This was the time that I was blessed to write and publish my first book: **"The Burnout Factor™ on Education: 7 Strategies to**

Sustain Your Leadership and Your Life". I've desired to be a published author since the 3rd grade when I wrote my very first play in elementary school. More than 30 years later, that goal was achieved. Doing so birthed my purpose of sharing my life journey for the benefit of others through writing. It was also at this time when my entrepreneurial endeavors grew. It has only been in retrospect that I realized that the entirety of my journey of resets was my PATHWAY TO PURPOSE. To understand that all I experienced has been *"for such a time as this"*.

Conclusion

I can only imagine your thoughts as you are reading about the multiple life altering resets I've experienced. I admit, it has been A LOT. There have been times that I questioned why I went through so many challenges, shifts and resets in my life. I soon realized that while my life journey is unique, I am not alone. All of us go through life challenges that have shifted our very existence. 2020 has and will continue to do that in the lives of many. As the beautiful Maya Angelou shares above, we can be changed by life's challenges but, it does not minimize who we are at our core and who we're meant to be. Despite my multiple life resets, I refused to allow it to discourage me and keep me knocked down. And, that is my supportive guidance to you. You are likely experiencing multiple resets in your life right now. I want you to know this is not the end, it is only the beginning. As is shared on a framed photo in my home:

**SUNSETS ARE PROOF THAT
ENDINGS CAN BE BEAUTIFUL**

Lastly, I want to speak directly to anyone who is struggling with fear right now about their financial future and professional lives. I know it's not easy. I know you are worried and afraid. I have been there. During my journey of resets, I spent many months in a place of worry and fear. Fear is real and something that so many are battling during this time of global shifting. It is something that many of us are battling on a daily basis.

No matter how strong we may feel in our leadership role, 2020 has shaken our confidence. This is the time when we must reach deep within to strengthen our resolve. We have worked years to build a level of resilience to allow us to survive even during this time. I am a testament that you can go through some of life's most difficult seasons and come out stronger, healthier and with greater peace. That you can lose everything you thought was important but, ultimately gain so much more.

Today, I am blessed to live a life of purpose and have greater joy, peace, and love in my heart than ever before. I've learned to appreciate the simplest things in life. Now, don't get me wrong – my journey was not easy. But, it was certainly worth it. As this year continues, I want to encourage you that no matter how challenging it gets, you can and will sustain. No matter what occurs over the next several months, please know your value and worth will NEVER change in God's eyes. And, just as He has done for me, He will give you the strength to persevere.

A few years ago, I purchased this t-shirt during a concert at my church. When I saw it, it spoke to the depths of my soul. It has become the theme for my life journey. Life has most certainly knocked me down. But, by God's grace I got back up. Each time healthier and stronger. So, that is my closing guidance to you. 2020 has prompted unprecedented change. 2020 has forever changed our lives. Yes, 2020 has knocked us down.. BUT WE WILL GET BACK UP!

Reflections

Take some time to reflect on when you've had to hit the reset button in your own life. We have all had times when our lives have dramatically shifted. No matter how difficult, the blessing is that we are still here. You are still here. That means that you can use those experience to move forward. Think about just how resilient you've been in your own life. You can do it again.

_____

_____

_____

_____

_____

_____

_____

_____

_____

_____

_____

My Plan to Hit the Reset Button and Embrace Resilience

1. What do you need to let go of in the past, to ensure you can better sustain in the present and move into the future? Are there any wounds you need to heal?

_____

_____

_____

_____

_____

_____

_____

2. How can you reframe what we are currently experiencing from a place of deficit to one of perseverance and resilience?

_____

_____

_____

_____

_____

_____

3. In this final question, I ask that you celebrate you. You've made it through one of the most challenging periods in our history. And will continue to do so. I am intentionally making this page a bit longer. Take the time to celebrate your perseverance and resilience. You are stronger than you realize. I send you blessings for continued sustaining power!

RECOMMENDED READING

1. "The Sleep Revolution: Transforming Your Life, One Night at a Time", by Arianna Huffington, April 4, 2017
2. "Relationship Goals: How to Win at Dating, Marriage, and Sex", by Michael Todd, Apr 28, 2020
3. "Mindfulness Meditations for Stress: 100 Simple Practices to Ease Tension and Find Peace", by Denise G. Dempsey MEd, Oct 6, 2020
4. "The Power of Your Subconscious Mind" by Joseph Murray, November 24, 2008
5. "Just Breathe: Leading Myself One Breath at a Time", by Renita Alexander, November 28, 2019
6. "The Four Agreements: A Practical Guide to Personal Freedom Part of: A Toltec Wisdom Book", by Don Miguel Ruiz, Nov 7, 1997
7. "The Power of No, Take Back Control and Find time For You", by Abbie Headon, 2019

CLIENT TESTIMONIALS

"Working with April Ervin through the pandemic and all that 2020 threw at us was an absolute blessing. April helped me to find the balance, strength, support, and focus that I needed in order to continue to lead during unprecedented times without losing myself or the mission in the process".
- *Amy Swann, CEO, Matchbook Learning*

"April's powerful spirit and passion for supporting leaders as they navigate stress, uncertainty, and imbalance is remarkable. Her commonsense coaching techniques are relevant and applicable. Our entire team grew from her coaching, leadership workshops, and more. If you're looking to put in the work, you'll grow in more ways than you can imagine."
- **Jasmin Shaheed-Young CEO, RISE Indy**

My coaching sessions with April were forward in thought, challenging, and often left our sessions feeling inspired, encouraged, and energized. Thank you for sharing your wisdom with the world, April!
- **Duane Ingram, Chief Operating Officer at SFI Risk Services**

ABOUT THE AUTHOR

April L. Ervin is founder and *Chief Peace Officer* of Sustainable Leadership, LLC – a mission-driven consulting firm dedicated to helping organizations sustain effective leadership and create healthy organizational cultures. She is committed to addressing the epidemic of burnout, imbalance and high turnover and prompt a paradigm shift toward strengthened leadership, empowered teams, and long-term sustainability. With 25 years of a diversity of leadership experiences, April intimately knows the challenges leaders face. Like far too many, she spent years working to the point of exhaustion sacrificing self for the sake of mission. She supports her clients see there is another way. That it is possible to serve your purpose AND live a healthy, balanced, fulfilled life. April is an avid believer that a more holistic approach to leadership development will have a transformative impact on the state of our world.

Her goal:

To help 1 million people eliminate burnout by the end of 2025.

April has private and public sector experience with roles in education nonprofit management, management consulting, investment banking and communications – receiving her undergraduate degree from Northwestern University and an MBA from the University of Michigan.

She is the author of *"The Burnout Factor on Education™: 7 Strategies to Sustain Your Leadership and Your Life"* and *"The Burnout Factor™ On Leadership: Managing Burnout in a Time of Unprecedented Change"*. Providing a step-by-step guide to help leaders move from chaos to calm, exhaustion to rejuvenation and burnout to professional and personal sustainability. She is a highly sought-out speaker and facilitator helping leaders achieve their purpose while also creating sustainable organizations.

CONTACT INFORMATION
April L. Ervin, MBA
Chief Peace Officer (CPO)
Sustainable Leadership, LLC
april@aprilervin.com
http://aprilervin.com/

www.EnhancedDNAPublishing.com
DenolaBurton@EnhancedDNA1.com